Azher Aslam

Contemporary Panopticism

Current social control

Anchor Academic
Publishing

Aslam, Azher: Contemporary Panopticism. Current social control, Hamburg, Anchor
Academic Publishing 2016

Buch-ISBN: 978-3-95489-487-1
PDF-eBook-ISBN: 978-3-95489-486-4
Druck/Herstellung: Anchor Academic Publishing, Hamburg, 2016

Bibliografische Information der Deutschen Nationalbibliothek:
Die Deutsche Nationalbibliothek verzeichnet diese Publikation in der Deutschen
Nationalbibliografie; detaillierte bibliografische Daten sind im Internet über
http://dnb.d-nb.de abrufbar.

Bibliographical Information of the German National Library:
The German National Library lists this publication in the German National Bibliography.
Detailed bibliographic data can be found at: http://dnb.d-nb.de

All rights reserved. This publication may not be reproduced, stored in a retrieval system
or transmitted, in any form or by any means, electronic, mechanical, photocopying,
recording or otherwise, without the prior permission of the publishers.

Das Werk einschließlich aller seiner Teile ist urheberrechtlich geschützt. Jede Verwertung
außerhalb der Grenzen des Urheberrechtsgesetzes ist ohne Zustimmung des Verlages
unzulässig und strafbar. Dies gilt insbesondere für Vervielfältigungen, Übersetzungen,
Mikroverfilmungen und die Einspeicherung und Bearbeitung in elektronischen Systemen.

Die Wiedergabe von Gebrauchsnamen, Handelsnamen, Warenbezeichnungen usw. in
diesem Werk berechtigt auch ohne besondere Kennzeichnung nicht zu der Annahme,
dass solche Namen im Sinne der Warenzeichen- und Markenschutz-Gesetzgebung als frei
zu betrachten wären und daher von jedermann benutzt werden dürften.

Die Informationen in diesem Werk wurden mit Sorgfalt erarbeitet. Dennoch können
Fehler nicht vollständig ausgeschlossen werden und die Diplomica Verlag GmbH, die
Autoren oder Übersetzer übernehmen keine juristische Verantwortung oder irgendeine
Haftung für evtl. verbliebene fehlerhafte Angaben und deren Folgen.

Alle Rechte vorbehalten

© Anchor Academic Publishing, Imprint der Diplomica Verlag GmbH
Hermannstal 119k, 22119 Hamburg
http://www.diplomica-verlag.de, Hamburg 2016
Printed in Germany

ACKNOWLEDGEMENTS

The process of this paper began in 2012 and has been by far the most challenging subject I have worked on. The journey I have been on both professionally and personally have impacted this paper in many ways from the research process to the final draft stage. In a short space of time I have met individuals who have impacted my thoughts and influenced the direction of this paper in ways I did not conceive or predict.

I would like to thank my family for their continued support throughout this lengthy process.

My close friends in particular my long friend Kashif Jamil and Mohammed Majid who always kept me on track both personally and professionally. Even at my lowest, you understood me beyond anyone and I will not forget that.

CONTENTS

ACKNOWLEDGEMENTS 5
ABSTRACT 9
INTRODUCTION 10
HISTORICAL ANALYSIS OF PANOPTICISM 11
CHARACTERISTICS OF PANOPTICISM 13
CONTEMPORARY SURVEILLANCE AND PRINCIPLES OF PANOPTICISM 16
INSTITUTIONAL SURVEILLANCE 27
SOCIAL MEDIA AND SURVEILLANCE 29
CONCLUSION 38
REFERENCES 39

ABSTRACT

The growth in surveillance has been a component of the growth of contemporary society, however, due to advances in information technology and the rise of greater links in communication there are other forms of surveillance, such as the internet and social media, which complicate methods of social control. The mix of advanced technologies supported by sufficient data management systems used by governmental agencies and corporate groups has provided a more undistinguishable and more powerful means of surveillance. Modes of social control have now developed into systems of control where an individual can be empowered and empower others. Living in a society where every movement whether online or while shopping on the local high street can be monitored and scrutinized leads to an environment where intrusion becomes an integral part of modern life. A life of surveillance is therefore sure to prevail. This paper discusses how contemporary surveillance has elements of the principles of panopticism in its processes. The discourse suggests that contemporary forms of control have some elements of discipline however principles of constant observation with constant scrutiny are highlighted to be a significant aspect of contemporary surveillance processes. Furthermore the paper highlights that contemporary surveillance, where data is power and having knowledge about individuals and groups by governmental agencies and corporations extends this power, collects its information reminiscent of panopticism.

INTRODUCTION

This aim of this paper is to argue that contemporary surveillance is a panoptic process. In order to do this, the paper will compare the principles of panopticism in contemporary surveillance methods to its origins in Victorian surveillance. It will be based around panopticism as panopticism is a key theory in understanding how power and control is distributed through the means of surveillance. The first section will be a historical analysis of surveillance focusing on how discipline, control and power through the means of surveillance, are embodied within the principles of panopticism. This section will also look at Victorian surveillance processes and how power and control was subjected on individuals and for what purpose. The second section will explore the concept of panopticism in terms of power, discipline and control. This section will critically analyse Michel Foucault's work on panopticism through the work of Gilles Deleuze, focusing on the panoptic principles of discipline and control. The third section will be a contemporary analysis of power and control within contemporary surveillance methods. This section will attempt to highlight that contemporary surveillance methods have large elements of panopticism within its processes. Due to limitations, this paper will focus on the contemporary surveillance methods of security and surveillance, Institutional surveillance and social media and surveillance.

HISTORICAL ANALYSIS OF PANOPTICISM

Before delving into the concept and principles of panopticism, it is important to understand the period in which it was developed. This would be useful in order to analyse the relevance of panoptic principles in Victorian society and furthermore its value in contemporary society. During the Victorian era there were many notable changes occurring in society such as political developments and cultural reform. Upper and middle classes wanted to separate themselves from the lower working classes such as labourers. This was done by instilling discipline to these labourers which was used in a manner to control them and keep them subjected to power (Andrzejewski, 2008). These labourers were cogs within the key change of this period, being the industrial revolution. The industrial revolution developed from an industrialisation boom resulting in a change from an agricultural focused society into asociety based on an economy of trade and manufacturing. This rapid growth of manufacturing led to a society of capitalism where efficiency of production became a key aspect of this growth. Efficiency of production was based on discipline of labourers (Andrzejewski, 2008).

Within a factory setting the labourers' were under constant surveillance by supervisors which ensured compliance to rules and regulations of the workplace and consequences were harsh if not compliant. In many instances the workers did not know they were being watched and therefore assumed they were always being watched (Mainwright, 2005). This constant observation was performed in order to gather information on the best workers and which labourers could be utilised best for the purposes of production (Clark, 1994). Supervisors noted down which workers performed and these observers also highlighted any room for improvement thus suggesting that the supervisors had the role of scrutinising where workers were not compliant. Where it was found that labourers were performing very well, these individuals were given longer breaks or given opportunity to gain more money through work. They were also encouraged to tell supervisors which workers are not working or causing disruption to the production process (Clark, 1994).Consequences of lack of compliance to performance standards or rules and regulations however, led to punishments which included lack of pay if the workers arrived late for their shift or talking while at work (Andrzejewski, 2008 and Clark, 1994). This ensured that the workers must arrive together and work together in a coordinated manner. This developed an internal discipline of time and mentality. Factory discipline was very important and the supervisor dictated the discipline in many ways. The supervisor told the workers when to work, how they conduct themselves during the job and make sure the jobs are being done within a reasonable time. Discipline was therefore designed to *"coerce workers into doing more work than they would freely choose to do had they maintained control of their hours of work and work intensity"* (Clark, 1994: 129). Discipline was used in a manner to increase potential for profit in order to gain as much as possible from an individual worker.

Following the above discourse, it is now possible to understand and analyse the inception of panopticism as a concept of surveillance. The above discourse will aid in understanding how principles of control and power are subjected on individuals and groups in contemporary surveillance methods.

CHARACTERISTICS OF PANOPTICISM

The panopticon is a type of building, such as a factory, hospital or school designed by English utilitarian Jeremy Bentham. The specific design of the building allowed an individual to observe many inmates of an institution without the inmates ever knowing they are being watched. The most analysed institution within the framework of the panopticon design is of a prison setting. It is difficult to theorize contemporary surveillance and panopticism without any confrontation from Michel Foucault's *'Discipline and Punish'* (1975) discourse. Foucault attempts to elaborate on the concept of panopticism and highlights the function of discipline as a mechanism within a prison. Furthermore he argues that discipline is used as a form of power against inmates. Foucault suggests that constant observation or perceived observation acts as a control mechanism where discipline is internalised leading to inmates becoming socially constructed identities which are considered 'norms' of society (Foucault 1975). Once discipline is internalised, the inmates conform to these 'norms' automatically; a concept called 'docile bodies' by Foucault. He also emphasized the importance of the principle that power should be visible and unverifiable where the supervisor or prison guard sees everything yet is never seen by the inmate. His analysis goes on to state that constant observation of the inmate allows to order and provide 'social sorting' of the inmates which allows constant scrutiny of the inmates behaviour and mannerisms. Once the inmates are individualised and are under constant observation, there are greater levels of efficiency within the prison which leads to an automatic functioning of power.

The theoretical analysis of Foucault's work on panopticism and particularly of his work on discipline is a key critique used by commentators such as Gilles Deleuze. Deleuze suggested that Foucault's work on discipline and control is not representative of post-modern societies and Deleuze's critique will form the basis of critique for the purposes of this paper. *"Postscript on the societies of control"* (1992) by Deleuze suggested a shift in society from a disciplinary society as stipulated by Foucault to a controlling society where individuals and the environment where they reside and work, become more complicated, diverse and technologically advanced. Deleuze suggests in his discourse regarding panopticism, that the spatial metaphor used by Foucault in his analysis of the panopticon, is no longer applicable in post-modern societies. Within the context of space, Deleuze suggests that discipline is highly reliant on its enclosures which operate as 'castings' or 'moulds'. These enclosures can be of various types; either physical, cultural or material (Deleuze, 1992).

Disciplined societies are societies where every individual has their own 'signature' however in post modern societies, Deleuze suggests that control and power needs to be understood in terms of open and fluid spaces (Simon, 2005: 15) highlighting that control and discipline does not act on the body so much as the environment through which the body moves (Simon, 2005: 15). Societies of control however modulate a body whereas societies of discipline attempt to objectify and stabilize bodies. The 'signatures' of an individual are different in societies of control and are not so much signatures but codes; codes acting as a password to access locations or services and therefore control mobility. Deleuze therefore highlights in his argument that an individual is doubled as code, as information or as simulation such that the metaphor of the panoptic gaze is no longer relevant to the physical body, but its 'coded' double.

Observation is therefore not a key indicator of surveillance in post-modern society, but of data analysis. Controlling societies emphasise 'information' about bodies and minds and not 'acting' on bodies and minds (Boyne, 2000). This emphasis on information about individuals according to Deleuze, produce a form of 'dataveillance' which parallel the modulating effects of power. These effects of modulating are occurring due to the potential of technology to produce and manage these 'data doubles' of individual citizens. These concepts towards the identification of an individual could never be matched by mere visual enclosure (Simon, 2005: 15). Disciplinary surveillance is designed to control the body and mind yet 'dataveillance' aims to control the representation of the body through data and statistical analysis. Deleuzes' argument towards to a society of control and not of discipline is further enhanced by other commentators such as Poster (1996) and Lyon (2003). Poster argues that these databases act as a 'superpanopticon' where information is sourced, sorted and organised, producing subjects of power. Lyon (2003) further suggests that controlling societies are potentially scarier than disciplinary societies. Lyon suggests that as greater amount of data is collected and administered regarding an individual, it is possible to gain an insight into the movements, actions, interests, eating habits or spending habits of that individual. This can then be assessed for various purposes such as national security or for gaining an edge within the realms of business for capitalist gain. This therefore leads to contemporary surveillance methods and its relevance to principles of panopticism.

CONTEMPORARY SURVEILLANCE AND PRINCIPLES OF PANOPTICISM

As David Lyon has pointed out, the sociological response to the general issue of surveillance has been dominated by images of the Panopticon (Lyon 1994). This has been especially true of CCTV surveillance which naturally invites comparisons with Jeremy Bentham's proposal, written in 1787, for an architectural system of social discipline, applicable to prisons, factories, workhouses and asylums. Bentham's architectural design "has been one of the most powerful metaphors in locating the theoretical and social significance of CCTV in contemporary society" (Norris 2003: 249). The design of the panopticon illustrates the mechanism of surveillance. It consists of a circular prison building including a central watchtower. It enables a single officer to control a multitude of prisoners. Its impressive clearness makes it an evident model for contemporary trends of surveillance. In form of modern CCTV systems – as for example in shopping malls – the panopticon suppose to celebrate its renaissance: The view of the camera's eye is expected to be felt by the subjects regardless of the operation or even the existence of a CCTV system. It is hardly surprising, then, given the parallels that can be drawn with CCTV, that many theorists have been drawn to both Foucault's concept of the Panopticon and his analysis of its disciplinary potential (see Davis 1990; Fyfe and Banister 1996; Reeve 1998).

As Fyfe and Bannister (1994) note, CCTV, like the Panopticon, facilitates the power of the watchers over the watched not only by enabling swift intervention to displays of non-conformity but also through the promotion of habituated anticipatory conformity. However, just taking the diversity of current forms of CCTV systems into account, it is obvious that the panopticon approach, stressing parallels to the industrial age of the 19th century, is highly questionable in regard to current social developments towards a post-industrial society based on mobility and information flows. Lyon considers: "Whatever one may learn from Jeremy Bentham's Panopticon or George Orwell's totalitarian telescreen technology, it is not clear if these are entirely helpful ways of understanding surveillance today." (Lyon 2002: 4). Thus McCahill states that one has to go "beyond Foucault" (McCahill 1999). Given the challenges of globalisation and the new patterns of living in a highly individualised society the panopticon has to be re-examined, combined with other discourses and models. Re-reading Foucault

Norris has lately extended the understanding of it. He pointed out that in the end the panopticon is "far more than anarchitectural form of visualization". It implies at its "heart" already "the collection of individualized codified information". As the deviant is segregated from society, the panopticon is "exclusionary" as well as "inclusionary". It provides a "rationale for social classification" (Norris 2003: 251).

A further strand is to interpret the increasing use of CCTV in the context of the contemporary shift towards a risk society (Beck 1986). Thus, a changing perception of security can be observed all over the world. New sources of insecurities are located in terrorism, drug trade, growing social inequalities, transnational migration or the vulnerability of information and communication infrastructure. In this context CCTV is understood as a response to risks. The multifunctional potential of it makes it a management tool for all kinds of dangers and possible hazards, such as traffic jams, fire, tunnel accidents, crime, terrorist attacks etc. In this respect a shift from reactive to proactive policing can be considered. Moreover, it has been pointed out, that the management of risks is not only addressed to state agencies as the police but increasingly to a mixture of institutions and organisations within the security branch. In combination with neo-liberal political programmes and strategies risk management becomes more and more a responsibility of corporate and individual regulation. (McCahill1999: 54) An installation of a CCTV system leads meanwhile probably in many countries of Europe to price deductions in insurance. The suicide plane attacks of September 11th have certainly roused a world-wide concern for issues of risk and increased the sense of insecurity. It is likely it has intensified the public acceptance for the further installation of CCTV throughout the world.

A further perspective of understanding the increasing use of CCTV is the current trend of commodification urban space. Its increasing employment is described as part of a broader transformation of contemporary cities throughout Europe. Within the reconstruction of the old industrial to the new post-fordist city, which is characterised not by a mixture of functions, but first by the management of leisure and consumption, CCTV is understood as a tool of economic restructuring space. Parallel to architectural revitalisation, declined city centres, e.g. around central stations, shall be "won back "through its employment. It is argued, that the aim is to create a 'commode' space for tourists and consumers. In times of scarce urban financial resources a new emerging understanding of urbanism is suspected to immolate public space for pure economic interest. Reeve considers: "The danger is that this largely insidious move towards a particular and commercially driven conception of what public space is for may lead to management and even policing practices which reduce the social richness of public space and thereby reduces its potential to be genuinely civilising and civic" (Reeve 1999: 73).

Turning away from the idea of urbanism in terms of social difference it is assumed that public space is transformed to homogenised zones. But the purpose of commodification is not just the creation of pleasing and comfortable atmospheres. Within the entrepreneurial city, it is said, that the managing of urban space means to classify people according to their economic purchasing power. According to this visual surveillance could become a tool of social exclusion. It is argued, that people could be sorted out by operators if their appearance and behaviour is not in accordance with the commercial utilisation of space. Hence would follow, the commodification of urban space implies its segmentation according to certain social affiliations, which are negotiated not publicly, but determined by commercial interests. In line with that, it is also seen that the commodification of urban space correlates secondly with an inner commodification of behaviour of those who want to belong to the favoured space. A certain behaviour and appearance is asked for in order to participate on the playground of leisure and consumption. Within this context the surveillance potential of CCTV turns out to be one of "social sorting" (Lyon 2003).

While surveillance can be perceived as monitoring of people's actions, the key characteristic that singularizes dataveillance is the type of monitoring; under surveillance, tactics of monitoring are more physical whereas dataveillance practices are digital. Particularly, dataveillance can express interest for the digital traces of a person as for example credit card transactions, phone calls, online activity and online purchases. Clarke identifies two types of dataveillance; *personal* and *mass dataveillance techniques*. (Clarke, 1988)

Personal dataveillance mechanisms are simply records that organizations/companies or institutions keep of individuals they are interested in, for purposes of determining whether their financial transactions for example are acceptable or valid. *Mass dataveillance mechanisms* are applied on a group of people when there is a certain interest in some of them. Those mechanisms are centred on verification of data, mostly again financial, while comparing them with data collected by other organizations/companies. For this to be achieved organizations use facilitative mechanisms via computer matching verification programmes. (Clarke, 1988). Even though surveillance is a phenomenon apparent for centuries, contemporary surveillance has managed to develop through time and technology and it is necessary to distinguish between the face of the surveillant. In this chapter focus will be given to the methods of surveillance towards individuals by the State which includes police, governments and State institutions/organizations. A number of scholars have dealt with that specific subject, and in order to explain the methods of surveillance by the State, I will concentrate on Marx (1985, 1988, 2002, 2003, 2004), Slobogin (2002, 2005), Wong (2006), Crampton (2007), Wood (2009) and Wright et al (2010).

Gary Marx in his article *"Are we becoming a Maximum Security Society"* (1985) identified the link between surveillance mechanisms and the end of privacy along with individual liberty. In his analysis of surveillance mechanisms, he refers to electronic devices that are commonly used to know the whereabouts of convicts (on parole). Several well-known devices used by police are taps, wires, polygraphs etc., and of course satellites, radars and others similar to those mentioned, which are generally used with the excuse of safety and precaution from unpleasant and deadly events such as terrorists attacks. In his view, society couldn't manage to see the negative side effects of such technological improvements and for the author this is quite risky because such acts should not be left aside. In his own words, *"privacy is also difficult to protect because much of the surveillance either is almost impossible to detect or truly invisible."* (Marx, 1985, LA Times) Consequently he states that there is a major need for attention to these new technologies and he underlines the need to adopt appropriate approaches to cope with those mechanisms infringing on privacy.

Few years following the publication of the above-mentioned article, Marx argued in another article entitled *"Make sure the video camera doesn't lie"* (1988) that since technology has involved in such way that videos of events are being used everywhere and represented quietly important evidence in criminal proceedings, people should be more thoughtful before believing what is actually on the video. Due to the high level of fabrication methods, falsifications may be included on the videos which means that privacy for one more time is of concern. In addition, he raises the matter of whether public cameras and importantly hidden cameras, affect our privacy rights:

"Do our privacy protection laws need to be changed to take account of the new situations created by video? Should videotaping, now largely exempt from legislation, be subject to the same legal requirements asaudio-taping, or to even more stringent standards, since it is more invasive?" (Marx, Newsday, October 23, 1988)

Moreover, in a 2002 article, Marx introduces the concept of New Surveillance as *"the use of technical means to extract or create personal data. This may be taken from individuals or contexts."* (Marx, 2002, p. 12) A list with examples is given following this definition, examples of everyday life where mechanisms of new surveillance are been used by lay people besides police; "children monitors", "video surveillance cameras on working environments" etc. (Marx., 2002, p. 13) With the clarification concerning the concept of new surveillance and along with the examples, it is clear that technological development offered to surveillance techniques new methods, that would make surveillance as a tactic more transparent to the individuals. The important fact is that even though concern is been raised regarding those techniques used by police and by ordinary people, laws and prohibitions should be more strict in order to ensure privacy and individual freedom of citizens.

Geosurveillance, according to Crampton (2007) is used by State to control territories, groups, populations and in extend individuals if necessary. Its techniques are varying among "tracking devices like radio frequency identification tags in passports, cell-phone geolocation, closed-circuit television, organ donors and the monitoring of criminals." (Crampton, 2007, p. 391) The justification behind this type of surveillance is the fear of terrorism and immigration. Immigrants are for decades a significant matter for states and via satellites and all those other techniques mentioned above, government is trying to regulate the amount of illegal immigrants passing borders or creating groups that could be a danger for the society, ergo fear for terrorism.

Wood (2009) examined the "fears" in U.S. that lead to those surveillance tactics. According to him, around 1960-70 U.S. government was afraid of two major phenomena; *"threat of communism"* and *"sexual revolution"* along with "*feminism.*"(Wood, 2009, p. 182) In response to those phenomena, surveillance tactics were adopted by U.S. Administration, in order to be able to control citizens with the preferable outcome to be aware of any plans or events prior their occurrence. Wiretapping and monitoring at the time were used by the military, the NSA and FBI but along came databases of personal information. (Wood, 2009) Consequently, this response of the state lead to a "*fear for the state*" (Wood, 2009, p. 182), a fear related to the acts of the State and its representatives would commit in order to ensure secrecy regarding government actions and safety for the U.S.

A decade later, wiretaps and monitoring gave their way to "*guidance systems, early warning and espionage satellites and resilient communications that could survive nuclear attack.*" (Wood, 2009, p. 183) Even though the methods adopted by the U.S were the first that raised concerns about privacy, the UK was the first country that installed CCTV monitoring in public spaces due to fear of hooliganism, and criminality levels. After this implementation by the UK other countries applied this technique to public places and it is more than clear that to some extent, Orwell's imaginary state has to a certain degree been successfully transposed from fiction into reality. As the State of Orwell's "1984" adopted monitors inside the house, in public etc. similarly States now all over the world adopted not only these kind of techniques but also profiling techniques, networks, databases, everything that a mind can think to control behaviours and thoughts and of course by extend prevent acts that are to be avoided.

Wright, Friedewald, Gutwirth, Langheinrich, Mordini, Bellanova, De Hert, Wadhwaa, Bigo (2010) argue that contemporary society is facing what they call "ubiquitous surveillance" and they identify three major characteristics of this new type of surveillance; "*the emergence of new image analysis algorithms in CCTV, the inclusion of new sensor systems that go beyond visual surveillance, and new data integration capabilities that combine traditional surveillance with advanced profiling and data mining techniques.*" (Wright, et al 2010, p. 346) Their definition of the term "ubiquitous surveillance" is the new face of surveillance that is at least unavoidable for every single individual since even the slightly transaction can be inspected; from daily shopping, to computer-internet browsing, consumer cards, DNA databases,

CCTV monitoring etc. Despite the existence of laws and declarations on invasion of privacy rights, surveillance tactics are part of in our daily lives.

The important thing that characterizes this new face of surveillance and distinguishes it from former types is the three features that are included. Firstly, as technology evolves through time, the potentials of CCTV monitoring are growing and its capabilities are becoming stronger. Some decades ago, CCTV monitoring was existent in public places but at this point everyone can monitor you, whether you are doing your shopping, walking on the street, watching a game at a football court, or even at your very private moments. Some examples of this phenomenon are the following; automated number plate recognition, activity recognition, facial recognition etc. (Wright, et al 2010, p. 348) Secondly, sensor systems might upgrade the quality of our lives but along with that, they can literally turn everything, even a building, into a transparent mass, making individuals identifiable from the outside. Such examples of innovations are the following; brain scanning, infrared non-contact temperature measurements etc. (Wright, et al, 2010, p. 349) Thirdly, data mining and process techniques are being intergraded and developed rapidly which makes the process of data proliferation easier. (Wright, et al 2010) Several examples of data integration are the following; location data mining, electronic health records and counterterrorism databases. (Wright, et al 2010, p. 350).

Surveillance by private sector includes techniques of categorization and profiling authorized by companies. Gandy (1993) chose to analyze surveillance regarding its impact on individuals. He introduced the term *"panoptic sort"* to describe a system where our personal information are gathered by companies and shared without our consent;

"The panoptic sort is a difference machine that sorts individuals into categories and classes on the basis of routine measurements. It is a discriminatory technology that allocates options and opportunities on the basis of those measures and the administrative models that they inform." (Gandy, 1993, p.15)

The three elements that are preluded are *identification, classification* and *assessment.* (Gandy, 1993) these are the processes of the panoptic sort and even though they are different, together they interact with a higher purpose; categorization of individuals. The first process, identification can be explained as the task of identifying the individual either via transactions, signature, fingerprint, DNA, face recognition, video or photograph. The second process, classification includes the categorization of individuals into certain categories based on the prior identification. For example, if you are consuming unhealthy food, smoke and drink then the system will categorize you as a risky person regarding health insurance policies based on expectations. If during the identification procedure there are gaps that are to fill in, then the system will try to fill them in by what is expected. It doesn't matter if you still haven't faced a serious disease; you are prone to develop diabetes. This is a sort of classification based on expectations. The third and final process is the assessment. During this stage individuals are assessed based on the two other processes and they are compared with others in order to create a hypothesis for each individual. (Gandy, 1993)

Stalder (2002) links surveillance to privacy as follows; consumers are inspected from their transactions by companies, banks, websites etc. All of the latter share a personal information database and unfortunately people cannot avoid sharing their data with them because on the contemporary society no one can remain in the shadows. Therefore he refers at this point to the matter of *"Bubble Theory of Privacy."* (Stalder, 2002, p.122) This means that even though citizens are discomforted by the sharing and processing of their personal data, most of them are doing nothing to alter the situation; people continue to share their data because as discomforted as this might be and despite the fact that there is a feeling of invasion of privacy, it is more than difficult to achieve any kind of transaction without sharing personal information. (Stalder, 2002)

The subject of panoptic surveillance is introduced by Elmer (2003) as he unfolds the routine of processing personal information of consumers. On Elmer's "A Diagram of Panoptic Surveillance", surveillance is apparent on a specific extension; consumer profiling.

"The removal of uncertainty, and by extension the need to make conscious decisions, is replaced by an uncannily familiar world of images, goods, and services. Such is the case with digital television and a host of techniques on the world wide web, where programming/content is sometimes automatically filtered down to reflect past viewing choices." (Elmer, 2003, p. 244)

In this passage it is more than obvious what Elmer cites; as technology is evolving, the uncertainty and the limited possibilities of individuals gave their way to certainty and solutions not only via interactive transactions but also via web pages and so on. Despite all that, he states that funder the panoptic surveillance, the essence of punishment and discipline are not implemented in society as they were on conceived for the Panopticon. On the contrary, punishment and discipline are being implemented differently. For example, when an individual is using web pages to proceed to his purchases, then several discounts and coupons are offered to him via those web pages. The latter can be characterized as reward. When the individual chooses to proceed to purchases not online but via physical transactions, then those discounts and coupons are not offered. Punishment here can be perceived as this particular withholding of reward; consumers are rewarded if they follow these new consuming techniques but they are punished only if they choose to stop using those at some point for any reason. Then and only then, punishment and need for discipline appear. It is essential at this point to clarify that the form of punishment is the inconvenience that consumers would face in their transactions. As consumers, we share with companies our personal data so they can provide for us the favorable reward based on our consuming level, but punishment only occurs when a change take place that affects the system generally. (Elmer, 2003).

Ericsen and Haggerty (1997) have suggested that since the attacks of September 11 and 2001, western societies have focused on public safety and security leading to these societies being highly concerned with risk and having centralised power, primarily from government bodies controlling such risks (Ericsen, Haggerty, 1997: 86). An objective of governance is to provide a strong level of security however levels of security are based on risk management. This is due to purposes of national and domestic security in order to manage threats (Webb, 2007). McCahill (1998) has also suggested that a change in threat management from focusing on the mental aspect such as criminal behaviour to focusing on the physical act such as behaviour which can be seen is now made possible (1998: 54). This therefore suggests that behaviour which is observed is used for the purpose of security; however it also has the power to directly manipulate behaviour. Risk management suggests risk is analysed based on information gained from the movement and observation of individuals. It is therefore possible to manipulate behaviour and movement along with the environment through such analysis. Therefore the rationale of this surveillance can be argued to scrutinise and manipulate the behaviour of individuals and this is also a key process of panopticism (King, 2001).

Security surveillance includes the form of CCTV (Closed Circuit Television) which uses different forms of power. A way in which CCTV uses this power is through an authoritative direct response such as when a security guard responds to an individual behaving in a manner which is not appropriate and then the guard, verbally or physically, attempts to stop the behaviour from occurring. There is therefore the constant potential of scrutiny (Ogura, 2006). CCTV is also used in a manner of deterrence where if an individual is aware of the presence of a CCTV, they would restrain their behaviour in order not to get caught. This allows for constant adherence to rules and regulations. One of the key forms of power subjected by CCTV's is to internalise its power of surveillance within the individual being observed and therefore reduce potential for further deviant behaviour. This suggests that due to CCTV, the fear of being caught or of scrutiny is such that an individual would automatically deter from such behaviour without thinking (Ogura, 2006). Surveillance is therefore exercised over an individual but also through an individual resulting in automatic conformity (Ball, Webster, 2003). This type of surveillance is for the purposes of domestic and national security so an individual is always under surveillance and therefore has no choice but to be subjected to this surveillance (Koskela, 2003 and Coleman, Sim, 2000). This suggests a coercive process similar to that of the labourers' in factory surveillance.

However Wood (2003) highlights that while Foucaults' panopticism principle highlights an individual being under a permanent gaze, the visual surveillance which is subjected on an individual by CCTV systems in urban public spaces, does not allow such unremitting observation on one individual as they can only observe within their field of sight. Furthermore Wood (2003) highlights that the focus on discipline by Foucault resulting in the regulation of collective behaviour is not present in contemporary society due to the vast amount of CCTV being present and explicit in urban spaces. This therefore suggests that its purpose is for gathering information of movement and not necessarily for changing behaviour which is a key function.

A recent field used against the perceived threat of terrorism is of biometrics (Bowyer, 2003). The breakdown of anonymity is a component of panopticism and biometrics allow such a breakdown. These fields of biometrics attempt to sort and categorise individuals where their personal information is captured through their behaviour and mannerisms and provides an opportunity for scrutiny of faces. This sorting and categorising is a principle of panopticism and is reflected in the surveillance practices on labourers by supervisors. Gray (2003) highlights that the face give clues to our thoughts which can't be hidden hence there is a larger potential for control (Gray, 2003: 324 and Haines, 2010). This type of technology therefore suggests a technologically advanced version of observation and controlling of information for purposes of risk management.

INSTITUTIONAL SURVEILLANCE

Once an individual purchases a product, orders a product or service, their actions are recorded digitally, referenced and tracked. As this process has an element of omnipresence and has consequences related to mechanisms of social control, it has comparisons to principles of panopticism. Foucault (1977: 198) highlights that the mechanisms of panopticism include language and sound where there is constant observation and noting of personal information. An increasing number of commentators such as Ericson and Haggerty (1997) and Lyon (2001), as well as Deleuze (1992) have suggested that the automatic disciplinary consequences highlighted by Foucault, is not reflected in consumer practices and moreover personal information is not coerced and importantly not disciplined into surrender. The information is rather freely given however in exchange for a perceived benefit or opportunity such as an exclusive product or service.

In contemporary society it is difficult for an individual not to be a consumer and therefore not be a part of institutional practices such as monitoring. Individuals must allow for personal information to be collected in order for granting of services or products including legal obligations such as 'Tax Returns' where an individual must by law, provide personal information (Culnan, 1993). Deleuze (1992) argued however that such institutions have the power to reward participation and punish those who do not participate accordingly, similar to panopticism. Different institutional practices have their own methods of extracting information with disciplining and punishment being used in different ways (Fussey, 2009). Marketing strategies however would encourage some consumers to provide information by adding extra incentive such as further discounts, which would serve as reward for sharing information. If a consumer is aware that their information is being collected, this then provides the options of 'opting' in or being punished for not providing information, such as a lack of discount on products. This highlights that individuals can be manipulated and controlled for the purpose of capital and revenue (Hayles, 2009). Furthermore this discourse reflects the 'reward' and 'punishment' aspects involved in surveillance practices of Victorian factories. Some services however do not give an option of 'opting in' and merely collect information as they go along such as online transactions, thus *"surveillance is permanent in its effects, even if it is discontinuous in its action"* (Foucault, 1977: 201).

Elmer (2003) therefore suggests that as discipline of prisoners is automated in the setting of the panopticon, technologies in contemporary society have the power to automatically collect personal information on an individual (2003: 237). Panoptic principles such as centrality of power are therefore present in this type of surveillance as well as actions being able to be scrutinised. This is highlighted by instances in contemporary society where emails and phone calls are now scanned for key words for purposes of risk management. Furthermore the attitudes and lifestyles of individuals outside of the workplace are increasingly being scrutinised by the organisations that employ them. Such scrutiny includes individuals being disciplined by their employees for non compliance where employees do not act in accordance to company regulations.

This is done in different ways due to various technological ways and one of these ways is through social media which leads to the next area of discussion which displays how principles of panopticism have been transferred into virtual spaces.

SOCIAL MEDIA AND SURVEILLANCE

Social media platforms such as 'Facebook' and 'Twitter' allow large user groups to generate and re-generate surveillance by using self made subject matter. This idea of an individual providing surveillance for themselves and being able to scrutinise others is reflective of the discipline subjected to labourers' in a factory setting and how this scrutiny is used as a form of control (Clark, 1994).

In *Surveillance Studies: An Overview,* David Lyon defines surveillance as "the focused, systematic and routine attention to personal details for purposes of influence, management, protection or direction" (2007:14). Typically, *surveillance* refers to an activity which enables the nation state, or capitalist formations like corporations, to manage a population (Gandy 1993; Ogura 2006). This conception of surveillance involves an asymmetry in which individuals are surveilled by structural entities, the balance of power overwhelmingly tipped in favour of the surveillor. However, individuals both comply with and resist surveillance, a dynamic referred to by Anthony Giddens as the "dialectic of control" (1982). For instance, accounts of "sousveillance" (Mann, Nolan, and Wellman 2003) involve repurposing surveillance equipment to watch the watchers, whether by capturing video of police brutality at a Critical Mass event or tweeting about a protest march in Egypt. Electronic communication technologies are intrinsic to contemporary surveillance activities, such as wiretapping telephone conversations, using infrared cameras to find individuals in hiding, tracking people with biometric data, creating databases to process and aggregate this information, and so forth (Nissenbaum 2010). Similarly, social media technologies can be used by companies, marketers, and governments to collect significant amounts of data about individual users. For example, the photo-sharing site Flickr aggregates user information with data collected by its parent site Yahoo! Networked banner advertisements track users across websites, creating detailed pictures of their actions and demographics. Third-party Facebook or iPhone applications may collect and disseminate still more personal data toactors outside these networks (Hull, Lipford, and Latulipe 2010). Helen Nissenbaum isolates three privacy issues surrounding social network sites. First, people use social media to disseminate information about themselves, such as writing intimate blog entries or posting pictures online, with potentially negative effects, including limiting future employment, housing, and so forth. Second, people post information about others, whether deliberately or inadvertently, through actions like tagging faces in a photograph or @replying on Twitter. Third, social network site owners aggregate and distribute information that users provide to the site (2010: 59–64). Social surveillance intrinsically involves the first two issues. While both *surveillance* and *sous-veillance* are good starting points with which to think about issues of power and privacy within social networks, they do not help us understand increasingly common situations in which people of relatively equal power are watching each other and acting on the information they find. While this behaviour has existed throughout history (Locke 2010), social media differs significantly from pre-digital interpersonal and mediated communication. Digital information is replicable, persistent, searchable, and scalable; it can be easily disseminated, copied, and accessed (Boyd 2010). In many communities, Facebook, with its 800 million users, is ubiquitous (Facebook 2011b). Moreover, social media sites are commercial and incorporate capitalist logics, such as self-promotion and celebrity(Marwick 2010). As a result, social media users engage in self-conscious identity construction to manage impressions, taking the real and potential audience into account (Ellison, Heino, and Gibbs 2006;Hodkinson and Lincoln 2008; Liu 2007; Papacharissi 2002). The implications of enormous databases of consensually-provided information like Facebook and Twitter with their correspondingly large potential audiences are significant, and still developing.

Several scholars have linked surveillance to social media (Albrechtslund 2008; Andrejevic 2005; Joinson2008; Lampe, Ellison, and Steinfield 2006; Tokunaga 2011). In the tradition of surveillance theory, Andrejevic's relatively early study of "lateral surveillance," though focused primarily on other methods by which individuals could "spy" on their peers such as people search tools, identified Friendster as a tool for investigating potential dates (2005). Albrechtslund, while concurring with Andrejevic overall, argued that this surveillance could be positive and empowering, framing it as playful and participatory (2008). These concepts have also been investigated by quantitative scholars. In a study of more than two thousand undergraduates, Lampe *et al.* identified *social searching* as a primary use of Facebook: using the site to learn more about friends, acquaintances, and classmates, distinct from *social browsing* in which the site is used to meet new people. Lampe framed social searching as relationship-building (2006). Joinson continued this approach in two surveys of

Facebook users which categorized "keeping in touch" as a major reason for using the site. Joinson concurred with Lampe et al.'s distinction between searching and browsing, and further argued that this category included a sizable amount of surveillance-related activities, or "virtual people watching" (Joinson 2008). A recent study by Tokunaga (2011) examined what he calls "interpersonal electronic surveillance." He identifies four differences between traditional surveillance and the "horizontal" nature of social surveillance. "Vertical," traditional surveillance demonstrates a symmetrical surveillance, presence of a strong hierarchical power structure, and the "potential for regulatory oversight," and has different reasons for gathering information (706). The rest of the study is focused primarily on the surveillance of romantic partners (see also Muise, Christofides, and Desmarais,2009) and concludes that Facebook can contribute to feelings of jealousy and create a "feedback loop, "increasing time on Facebook.

Social surveillance clearly differs from traditional surveillance, to the point where some might question whether it is surveillance at all. Returning to Lyon's definition, social surveillance certainly involves "the focused, systematic and routine attention to personal details" that characterizes traditional surveillance. While surveillance is typically undertaken to manage, control, or influence a particular population, social surveillance leads to *self*-management and direction on the part of social media users. The internalization of the surveilled gaze—behavior modification as the result of being watched—can best be understood through the lens of surveillance studies. This paper fleshes out some of the tensions and complications in this perspective.

Social surveillance is the ongoing eavesdropping, investigation, gossip and inquiry that constitutes information gathering by people about their peers, made salient by the social digitization normalized by social media. It encompasses using social media sites to broadcast information, survey content created by others, and regulating one's own content based on perceptions of the audience. It can exist either within a particular social media site (e.g. Facebook) or across a variety of sites (e.g. Twitter, YouTube, and Foursquare). Social surveillance can be distinguished from other types of surveillance by the following characteristics:

- *Power:* Social surveillance assumes a model of power flowing through all social relationships.
- *Hierarchy:* Social surveillance takes place between individuals, rather than between structural entities and individuals.
- *Reciprocity:* People who engage in social surveillance also produce online content that is surveilled by others.

Power

In dualistic, judicial, or modernist notions of power, a large entity such as a government or corporation acts on a less-powerful actor. This hierarchical model of power is modelled after the right of the sovereign to impose his will onto his subjects, specifically the right to live or die (Foucault 1990; Gerrie 2007). In this concept, power is something possessed by an authority that is "exerted over things" which can "modify, use, consume, or destroy" (Foucault 1982, 786). Michel Foucault proposed an alternate model of power as micro-level, decentralized and present in all human relationships. He theorized "capillaries of power" that flow between networks and individuals. In this model, power is ever-present, fluid, and at work in the mundane day-to-day activities that make up human life (Foucault 1977; Foucault 1982). For example, gender norms are determined not by a patriarchy seated around a table, but through millions of interpersonal moments in which "masculinity" or "femininity" is reinforced, policed, or resisted (Butler1990).In this model, the individual is part of a push-pull interaction in which power is negotiated.

In traditional models of surveillance, power flows from the surveyors (government or corporate actors) to the surveyed. For instance, David Lyon writes:

Whatever the purpose of surveillance, to influence, manage, protect or direct, some kind of power relations are involved. Those who establish surveillance systems generally have access to the means of including the surveilled in their line of vision, whether that vision is literal or metaphorical. It is they who keep the records, hold the tapes, maintain the databases, have the software to do the mining and the capacity to classify and categorize subjects. Whether it is the massive Department of Homeland Security in the USA or some rural school board with cameras in buses, power is generated and expressed by surveillance (2007: 23).

Clearly this concept does not wholly capture the dynamic in situations where individuals both have access to the same tools and are able to mutually watch each other, as in two "friends" on Facebook or Foursquare. Nathan Jurgenson and George Ritzer refer to this type of power as the "omniopticon," in which "the many watch the many" (Jurgenson 2011).

In social surveillance, social media sites are a type of capillary through which power flows not only from the site to users, but between users and across networks. Thus, while both forms of surveillance are intrinsically dependent on power relations, social surveillance incorporates the power differentials inherent in individual relationships.

Hierarchy

Surveillance in its most commonly used form implies a significant power imbalance between the group gathering information and the group being watched. Typically, the group gathering information has *structural* or systemic power (Boyd 2011). This notion of extreme asymmetry does not capture the case of social surveillance, which is typically between peers of similar social status. However, Foucault's model of "capillaries of power" implies that power is constantly in flux between individuals. For instance, while we may idealize romantic relationships as egalitarian partnerships, at any one time one member of a couple may be wealthier, better looking, more or less jealous, in a bad mood, or far away—which can all affect the balance of power within a relationship. Although the consequences of these ebbs and flows are not the same as those between a corporation and an individual, or the state and an individual, they are no less significant to the individual. Indeed, individuals may care more about their relationships with romantic partners, family members, and close friends than they do about a nebulous corporate entity collecting personal information. Moreover, the use of the term "friends" to define connections on many social network sites flattens what may be very real power differentials based on social roles, such as boss/employee, teacher/student, or parent/child (Boyd 2006).

While traditional models of surveillance include individuals surveilled by hegemonic power structures or individuals surveilling structural entities in order to resist hegemonic power, social surveillance conceptualizes both sets of actors as individuals. This echoes the way social software flattens all relationships into a single category, and distinguishes social surveillance from other forms of surveillance that utilize social media. For instance, a Farmville-like game launched by a corporation in order to systemically gather information about people who play it does not constitute social surveillance, although the data-gathering takes place within Facebook. Rather, it falls into the category of "dataveillance" in that the corporation is an entity gathering information on individuals. Similarly, a government agent impersonating a Twitter user to investigate a drug deal does not constitute social surveillance, as the agent represents the state: the Federal Bureau of Investigation.

Social surveillance thus recognizes models of hierarchy that incorporate very real power differentials that exist beyond state/subject or corporation/consumer, based on social status, race, class, gender, social roles and so forth. While social surveillance exists between individuals, these individuals are not necessarily "equal" although they do not represent structural entities. Moreover, there are moments of slippage where a person's social role—as a parent, employee, or romantic partner— comes into unanticipated play. For instance, a Facebook user may complain about his work, forgetting that his boss is a "friend." This suggests that the division between "individual" and "entity" is not as distinct as traditional models of surveillance might have us believe. Taking social, rather than structural, hierarchy into account allows to account for such complexity.

Reciprocity

Social surveillance takes place between members of social media sites. People who use applications like Twitter and Facebook become part of a networked audience where participants both send and receive social information (Marwick and Boyd 2011). As a user skims her Facebook feed, she may simultaneously read her friends' content, comment on it, and broadcast her own content to other people's feeds, using this information to improve her mental model of other people's identities, actions and relationships. Social surveillance thus indicates that those who practice it are simultaneously surveilled by others. This differs from the asymmetry present in social media sites when users are watched by powers that they cannot watch back, such as marketers or data-miners. Although sharing information with others through social media is often framed as a form of exhibitionism, in reality, it is often motivated by trust and intimacy. Studies show that electronic communication is primarily used to reinforce pre-existing relationships, especially by young people (Boneva and Quinn2006; Gross 2004; Subrahmanyam and Greenfield 2008).

Social network sites, which require personal information, facilitate the maintenance of weak ties, strengthen friendships, and increase social capital and popularity (Christofides, Muise, and Desmarais 2009; Ellison, Steinfield, and Lampe 2007; Joinson 2008;Livingstone 2008). Many technologies, including social media, mobile phones, and instant messenger, are crucial to strengthening both individual and peer group relationships. Similarly, micro-blogging sites like Twitter encourage "digital intimacy" (Thompson 2008), reinforcing connections and maintaining social bonds (Crawford 2009). Unlike user-generated content sites like YouTube or Wikipedia, where a small percentage of users create the majority of the content, social network users do not just watch: they broadcast.

Again returning to Foucault's model of *capillaries of power,* social surveillance explains how power is internalized and used for self-discipline and impression management. In social media sites, users monitor each other by consuming user-generated content, and in doing so formulate a view of what is normal, accepted, or unaccepted in the community, creating an internalized gaze that *contextualizes* appropriate behaviour (Trottier 2011). Facebook users, for instance, imagine how readers will view their profile pictures and Wall posts and alter them accordingly.

As these social media platforms such as 'Twitter' are business related organisations, one could argue that their prime objectives are based on capital and revenue similar to the objectives of Victorian society. It attempts to achieve these objectives through calculated marketing schemes by aiming to analyse the personal information provided by the users of these platforms and therefore assessing which services or products to aim at certain groups or individuals. This type of surveillance is highly individualised therefore every user is targeted and distinguished. Similar to institutional surveillance, personal information is provided by the user willingly with no form of coercion therefore the user has the power to distribute their information as they please.

Gandy (1993) however has suggested that the 'tactics' of discipline are still enforced regardless of a lack of coercion. He argues that this type of 'panoptic sorting' organises every individual into specific groups in a manner similar to categorisation and therefore social media platforms are a system of power and a subject of surveillance with disciplinary aspects (Gandy, 1993: 15). Panoptic principles suggest that an individual under surveillance *"is the object of information and never a subject of communication"* (Foucault, 1977: 200). As social media platforms provide a foundation where masses of users can share information which can be communicated in an instant they are both objects of information and subjects of communication suggesting this principle is arguably not wholly applicable within this form of surveillance. However as interactions on such platforms are arbitrated by business related organisations, one can argue that these communication subjects become objects of information for these organisations and the state in processes of observation and scrutiny, example being, where governmental bodies such as the police force use social media for purposes of criminal investigation.

In context of social media platforms therefore, the power by business related organisations and the state is exerted through the accumulation and analysis of personal information provided by such platforms. The worldwide interaction of users generates the interest of these capitalist organisations to apply power over such interactions. Such developed levels of communication provide the overseers of power such as the state, to attain a greater understanding of the needs, wants and interests of users not for purposes of discipline but for controlling of information (Dinev, Hart, Mullen, 2008 and Jones, 2000).

There are aspects of social media platforms however which have disciplinary aspects as well differing from principles of panopticism which highlights that the metaphor of panopticism can still bear resemblance in modern surveillance. Andrejevic (2005) suggests that social media surveillance is peer to peer rather than 'agents' of control therefore power relations are not centralised from one source however Albrechtslund (2008) argues that Andrejevic transfers the power relations from the panopticon to the peer to peer monitoring. Even though the power relation is not centralised, users can still be scrutinised from 'a higher power'. This suggests that power structures have been diversified from one agent of power (the state) to several agents of power (social network users) however a 'higher power' still regulates control.

As the users are being observed and have the power to be the observers, they have the ability to scrutinise each other, either to each other or through the complaints system of the social media platform. Scrutiny is exercised in different ways. Users on such social media platforms can be punished if users use inappropriate language such as racist remarks (Notley, 2008). These punishments are exercised by other users, as well as administrators who manage communication's, by making complaints about comments and user pages (Lyon, 2006). The administrators of the platform have the ability to control what information is acceptable and therefore highlights both disciplinary and controlling aspects of social media platforms. This reflects the discourse on factory labourer's previously discussed and specifically how users can be disciplined through reward and punishment for compliance and non compliance of behaviour. Where an individual wants access to a specific page with privileged access, they must allow the social media platform to use their information for commercial purposes (Hamelink, 2000 and Lyon, 2006). This reflects the surveillance practice of institutional surveillance and specifically that of 'reward' and how capital and revenue is generated through that gathering of personal information and importantly the manipulation of personal information for purposes of capital.

CONCLUSION

"not only are we put to work inside the factory, but we are also put to work at home. We have been disciplined into spending our leisure time acquiring material goods and spending money in order to feed the capitalist economy" (King, 2001)

The above discourse suggests that panoptic principles are in existence within contemporary surveillance practices. The key panoptic principles of observation, scrutiny, conformity and control were all principles of panopticism and this paper suggests that these principles are still exercised in relation to the origin of panopticism in Victorian society. Furthermore the paper highlights that contemporary surveillance practices attempt to control the information about individuals and further control the environment where an individual moves. This therefore suggests that where panopticism attempts to control the body through discipline, the panoptic principles of contemporary society attempt to control the information about the body to manipulate its actions. Hence contemporary surveillance is attempting to structure the lives of those observed and therefore indirectly manipulate them. Contemporary methods of surveillance also have some aspects of disciplinary aspects where the mind is attempted to be manipulated such as the use of CCTV however the discourse suggests that discipline is not a key aspect of contemporary surveillance. The paper highlights that capitalism is an important aspect of surveillance and its comparison to Victorian surveillance practices suggests that there is a strong relationship between contemporary surveillance and capitalism.

REFERENCES

Albrechtslund, A. (2008) 'Online Social networking as participatory surveillance' *First Monday* 13 (3)

Andrejevic, M. (2005) 'The work of watching one another: Lateral Surveillance, Risk and Governance' *Surveillance and Society* 2 (4), 479-497

Andrzejewski, A, V. (2008) *Building Power. Architecture and Surveillance in Victorian America.* Knoxville: The University of Tennessee Press

Ball, K., Webster, F. (2003) *The intensification of surveillance.* London: Pluto Press

Bowyer, K., W. (2003) *Face Recognition Technology And The Security Versus Privacy Tradeoff* [online] available from.<http://molar.crb.ucp.pt/cursos/1%C2%BA%20e%202%C2%BA%20Ciclos%20%20Lics%20e%20Lics%20com%20Mests/Inform%C3%A1tica%20de%20Gest%C3%A3o/2%C2%BA%20Semestre/%C3%89tica%20e%20Deontologia/Papers%20para%20%C3%89tica/Face%20Recognition%20Technology%20And%20The%20Security%20Versus%20Privacy%20Tradeoff.pdf> [23rd July 2011]

Boyne, R. (2000) Post-Panopticism.*Economy and Society*, 29: 285-307.

Clark, G. (1994) 'Factory Discipline' *The Journal of Economic History* 54 (1), 128-163

Coleman, R., Sim, J. (2000) 'You'll Never Walk Alone: CCTV surveillance, order and neo-liberal rule in Liverpool City Centre'. *British Journal of Sociology,* 51 (4), 623-639

Culnan, M., J . (1993) 'How Did They Get My Name? An Exploratory Investigation of Consumer Attitudes Toward Secondary Information Use'.*MIS Quarterly*17 (3), 341-363.

Deleuze, G. (1992) 'Postscript on the Societies of Control'. *MIT Press* 59, 3-7

Dinev, T., Hart, P., Mullen, M.R. (2008) 'Internet privacy concerns and beliefs about Government surveillance. An empirical investigation' *The Journal of Strategic Information Systems* 17 (3), 214-233

Ericsen, R., V., Haggerty, K., D. (1997) *Policing the risk society.* Oxford: Oxford University Press

Elmer, G. (2003) 'A Diagram of Panoptic Surveillance'. *New Media and Society* 5 (2), 231-247

Foucault, M. (1977) *Discipline and Punish: The Birth of the Prison.Trans. by Alan Sheridan.* New York: Vintage

Foucault, M. (1975) *Discipline and Punish: The Birth of the Prison.* New York: Vintage

Fussey, P. (2009) 'Control and the Community: The Spread of Surveillance in the Post-Industrial City'. *Surveillance and Society* 4 (3), 229-256

Gandy, O. (1993) *The Panoptic Sort: A Political Economy of Personal Information.* Boulder: Westview.

Gray, M. (2003) 'Urban surveillance and panopticism: Will we recognize the facial recognition society?' *Surveillance and Society* 1 (3), 314-330

Haines, A. (2010) 'Vehicle surveillance in the UK: Big Brothers little Brother or little Brothers Big Brother?' *Social Criminology* 2 (2), 143-166

Hamelink, C., J. (2000) *The ethics of cyberspace.* California: Sage

Hayles, N., K. (2009) 'Waking up in the Surveillance Society' *Surveillance and Society* 6 (3), 313-316

Jones, R. (2000) 'Digital rule: Punishment, control and technology'. *Punishment and Society* 2, 5-22

King, L. (2001) 'Information, Society and the Panopticon' *The Western Journal of Graduate Research* 10 (1), 40-50

Koskela, H. (2003) "Cam Era'- The contemporary urban panopticon'. *Surveillance and Society* 1 (3), 292: 313

Lyon, D. (2003) 'Surveillance as social sorting: Computer codes and mobile bodies', *Surveillance as Social Sorting: Privacy, Risk and Digital Discrimination.* ed. by Lyon, D. London: Routledge, 13-30

Lyon, D. (2006) 'Synopticon and Scopophilia: Watching and being watched'. In Haggerty, K., D., Ericsen, R., V. (eds.) *The New Politics of Surveillance and Visibility.* Toronto: Toronto University Press

Lyon, D. (2001) *Surveillance Society: Monitoring everyday life.* Buckingham: Open University Press

Mainwright, E, M. (2005) 'Dundee's Jute Mills and Factories: Spaces of Production, Surveillance and Discipline' *Scottish Geograpical Journal* 121 (2), 121-140

McCahill, M. (1998) 'Beyond Foucault: towards a contemporary theory of surveillance' in *Surveillance, Closed Circuit Television and Social Control.* ed. by Norris, C., Moran, J., Armstrong, G. Aldershot: Ashgate: 41-65

Notley, T., M. (2008) 'Online network use in schools: Social and Educational opportunities' *Youth Studies Australia* 27 (3), 20-29

Ogura, T. (2006) 'Electronic Government and Surveillance-orientated'. In *Theorizing Surveillance: The Panopticon and Beyond.* ed. By Lyon, D.Cullompton: Willan

Poster, M. (1996).'Databases as Discourse; or, Electronic Interpellations'. In *Computers, Surveillance, and Privacy*. Ed. By Lyon, D, Zureik, E. Minneapolis, University of Minnesota Press: 175-192.

Simon, B. (2005) 'The return of panopticism: Supervision, subjection and the new surveilance' *Surveillance and Society* 3 (1), 1-20

Webb, M. (2007) *Illusions of Security: Global Surveillance and Democracy in the post 9/11 world.* San Francisco: City Light Books

Wood, D. (2003) 'Editorial. Foucault and panopticism revisited' Surveillance and Society 1 (3), 234-239